The University of Chicago

THE UNIVERSITY OF
CHICAGO

Photographed by Dan Dry

Harmony House

Publishers-Louisville

West window, Hutchinson Commons

Executive Editors: William Butler and William Strode

Library of Congress Catalog Number: 90-81394

Hardcover International Standard Book Number: 0-916509-67-2

Printed in the Republic of Korea by Sung In Printing Company, Ltd.

through Vivid Color Separation, New York, N.Y.

First edition printed Spring 1992 by Harmony House Publishers,

P.O. Box 90, Prospect, Kentucky 40059 (502)228-2010/228-4446

Copyright © 1992 by Harmony House Publishers

Photographs copyright © 1992 by Dan Dry

CONTENTS

Foreword   Page 15

A University Chronology   Page 18

"Recollections: A Few Midway Memories"   Page 97
by Edward W. Rosenheim

FOREWORD

Historian Frederick Rudolph has written that "no episode was more important in shaping the outlook and the expectations of American higher education . . . than the founding of the University of Chicago, one of those events in American history that brought into focus the spirit of an age."

It was an age that saw the foundation of the American research university, and it was Chicago that truly shaped that institution for our time and for the future. The University's founder was John D. Rockefeller, who was convinced by Yale Semitic scholar and fellow Baptist, William Rainey Harper, to support an institution that would be not only a college and not only a research institute but a fully formed university, where the primary mission would be research—discovery that would inform teaching. Its first faculty of 103 scholars included eight college presidents that Harper, the first president, recruited. Classes began on October 1, 1892, with an enrollment of 594 students. It was coeducational from the beginning and had no restrictions regarding the diversity of its student body or faculty. Before the development of the great state universities, it was the leading producer of black Ph.D.s among the elite institutions of higher education in the nation. Its students became the teachers at colleges and universities across the country and the world. Today at least 30 percent of its graduates enter fields of education, the highest proportion of any similar institution in this country, thus reinforcing its reputation as the "teacher of teachers."

From its very beginning, Chicago's campus was planned, and that plan was adhered to, with only a few departures during its first one hundred years. Henry Ives Cobb, the first architect chosen by the new

The Main Quadrangles

Board of Trustees, selected a form of late English Gothic, dividing the site, at that time a swamp, into six quadrangles, each surrounded by buildings, with the Main Quadrangle, the seventh, in the center. Charles E. Jenkins, writing in *Architectural Record,* described the reasons for the plan,

> to . . . exclude all outside conditions from the student when he once entered the University grounds . . . in fact, to remove the mind of the student from the busy mercantile conditions of Chicago and surround him by a peculiar air of quiet dignity which is so noticeable in old university buildings. When the quadrangles are completed this will be very marked, and, as this style of English Gothic architecture easily takes on an air of age by the help of a few vines and weather stains, the effect will certainly be most restful and suggestive of university conditions.

That is how it is today on the 175 acres of quadrangles and plantings, even across the Midway Plaisance on the South Campus dominated by the buildings of the modernists and in the newest, the Science Quadrangle. Chicago's campus is an architectural representation of the cohesive and connective nature of the University envisioned by the founder and its first president and carried through by their successors— faculty and students of each generation.

A UNIVERSITY CHRONOLOGY

1865   Chicago Baptist Theological Institute (Divinity School's forerunner) chartered

1889   John D. Rockefeller pledged initial $600,000 for University if an additional $400,000 could be raised within a year

1890   First meeting of the University's Board of Trustees; University of Chicago chartered

1891   Architect Henry Ives Cobb presented campus plan; William Rainey Harper assumed office as first president; William Rainey Harper bought Berlin collection, foundation of University Library

1892   First day of classes began in Cobb Hall, first campus building; University of Chicago Press incorporated; Alice Freeman Palmer named first dean of women

1893   Snell Hall opened; Eiji Asada received first Ph.D. (Semitic Languages & Literatures)

1894   Ryerson Physical Laboratory and Kent Chemical Laboratory dedicated

1897   Haskell Oriental Museum (now Haskell Hall) dedicated; Hull Biological Laboratories dedicated; Yerkes Observatory founded

1902   Charles L. Hitchcock Hall completed

1903   Theodore Roosevelt laid cornerstone for old Law School (now Stuart Hall); Mitchell Tower dedicated

1904   Frank Dickinson Bartlett Gymnasium dedicated; first Blackfriars production, "The Passing of Pahli Khan"

1906   William Rainey Harper died in his 15th year as president, at the age of 50

1907   Harry Pratt Judson elected second president

1911   West Tower of Harper Library collapsed during construction

1912   William Rainey Harper Memorial Library dedicated

1915   Rosenwald Hall dedicated; cornerstone laid for Ida Noyes Hall; Hiram Kelly Memorial (now Classics Building) dedicated

1916   Ida Noyes Hall dedicated with "Masque of Youth"

1920   School of Social Service Administration established

1923   Ernest DeWitt Burton elected third president; Lorado Taft's *Fountain of Time* dedicated

1925   Cornerstone laid for Joseph Bond Chapel; University Chapel (now Rockefeller Memorial Chapel) groundbreaking; Max Mason assumed office as fourth president

1926   Swift Hall dedicated; Joseph Bond Chapel dedicated

Aileronde, *by Antoine Poncet, 1973, in front of the*
Cummings Life Science Center

1928   Wieboldt Hall dedicated; Rockefeller Memorial Chapel dedicated; official U of C flag adopted

1929   Robert M. Hutchins inaugurated as fifth president; Social Science Research Building dedicated

1930   First baby delivered in Chicago Lying-in Hospital; Bobs Roberts Memorial Hospital dedicated

1931   New Plan for the College curriculum accepted by College faculty; Chicago Lying-in Hospital dedicated; Oriental Institute dedicated

1932   Graduate School of Education (now Charles Hubbard Judd Hall) dedicated; International House dedicated; Laura Spelman Rockefeller Carillon dedicated; first carillon recital

1935   Jay Berwanger, A.B. '36, received first Heisman Trophy

1938   Harriet Monroe Library of Modern Poetry opened; first Awards for Excellence in Undergraduate Teaching (now the Llewellyn John and Harriet Manchester Quantrell Awards) presented to William Thomas Hutchinson, Joseph Jackson Schwab, and Reginald Joseph Stephenson

1942   First controlled self-sustaining nuclear chain reaction achieved under west stands of Stagg Field by Enrico Fermi and his colleagues

1945   First issue of *Bulletin of the Atomic Scientists* published

1951   Research Institutes Building dedicated; Lawrence A. Kimpton inaugurated as sixth president

1959   Charles Stewart Mott Building dedicated; Goldblatt Pavilion dedicated

1960   Laird Bell Law Quadrangle dedicated

1961   First U of C Folk Festival opened; George W. Beadle inaugurated as seventh president

1965   School of Social Service Administration Building dedicated

1966   Silvain and Arma Wyler Children's Hospital dedicated

1968   Pritzker School of Medicine named; new Stagg Field dedicated; Edward H. Levi inaugurated as eighth president

1970   Joseph Regenstein Library dedicated

1971   Ben May Laboratory for Cancer Research dedicated

1973   Cummings Life Science Center dedicated

1976   John T. Wilson installed as ninth president

1977   Henry Crown Field House rededicated

1978   Hanna H. Gray inaugurated as tenth president

1984   Bernard Mitchell Hospital dedicated; John Crerar Library dedicated

1985   Samuel Kersten, Jr., Physics Teaching Center dedicated

1987   D'Angelo Law Library expansion and renovation dedicated

Pages 22-23: Linné, *by Johan Dyfverman, 1891*

The C-Bench

Hull Court, from the south

Pages 30-31: Judson dining hall in Burton-Judson Courts, from the library alcove

Botany Pond

Pages 32-33: David Tracy, the Andrew Thomas Greeley and Grace McNichols Greeley Distinguished Service Professor, Divinity School

William Rainey Harper Memorial Library and the Quadrangles

*Above, through page 45: Students sleep out on the Quadrangles to enroll
in their favorite classes*

Pages 46-47: Harold Leonard
Stuart Hall

45

*Looking across the Midway from the Harold J. Green Lounge
in the D'Angelo Law Library*

The D'Angelo Law Library

*Karl Weintraub, the Thomas E. Donnelley Distinguished
Service Professor, Department of History, teaches a
Western civilization class that students sleep out for*

Merton Miller, the Robert R. McCormick Distinguished Service Professor, Graduate School of Business, and 1990 Nobel laureate in economic sciences

Charles Lipson, Associate Professor, Department of Political Science

Amy Kass, Senior Lecturer, Humanities Collegiate Division

James Cronin, University Professor, Department of Physics, and 1980 Nobel laureate in physics

Dolores Norton, Professor, School of Social Service Administration

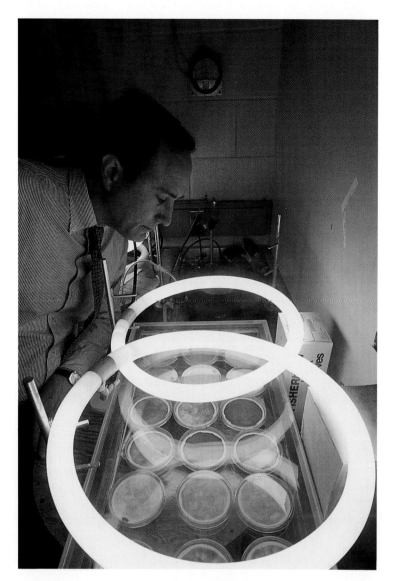

Robert Haselkorn, the Fanny L. Pritzker Distinguished Service Professor, Departments of Molecular Genetics & Cell Biology, Biochemistry & Molecular Biology, and Chemistry

Elizabeth Helsinger, Professor, Department of English Language & Literature

A class at Midway Studios

Goodspeed Hall music practice room

The Shaler Memorial Angel, *by Lorado Taft, 1923*

Construction in Space in the Third and Fourth Dimension, *by Antoine Pevsner, 1963*

Nuclear Energy, *by Henry Moore, 1967, at the site of the first controlled self-sustaining nuclear chain reaction*

*Detail from dining room ceiling,
Robie House*

Robie House, designed by Frank Lloyd Wright

The David and Alfred Smart Museum of Art

Assyrian winged bull, Oriental Institute Museum

Hull Court Gate

Wieboldt Arch

Joseph Bond Chapel

William Rainey Harper Memorial Library

59th Street METRA Station

Promontory Point at 55th Street and Lake Michigan

Downtown Chicago

Pages 68-69: The City of Chicago, looking west from the Sears Tower

Pages 70-73: Graduate School of Business dinner dance at the Field Museum of Natural History

Pages 74-75: Crew team on Lincoln Park Lagoon

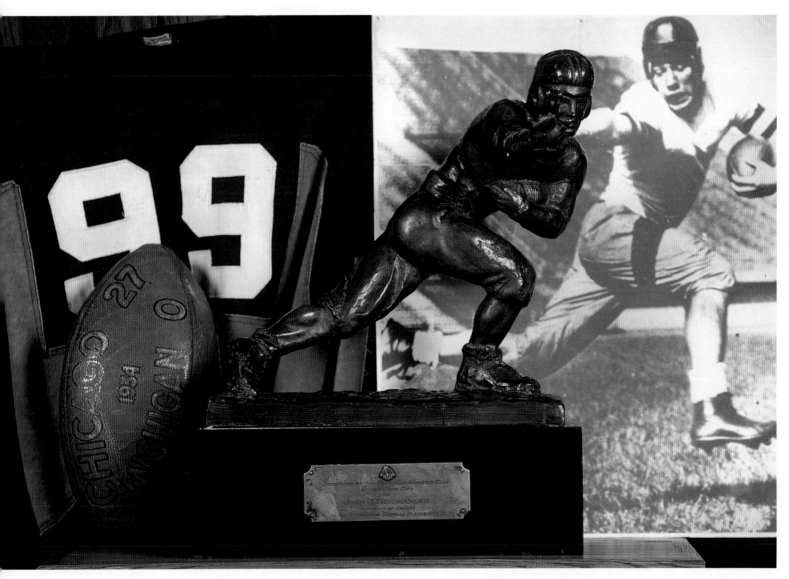

The first Heisman Trophy, modeled after its winner, Jay Berwanger, A.B. '36, shown in the background photo

Pages 80-81: The Midway Plaisance

Unaccompanied Women, a capella singers

Pages 82-83: Opera performance in Hutchinson Court

Interfraternity Sing at Mandel Hall

Bruce Tammen, Director (top, page 87), rehearsing
the Motet Choir in Goodspeed Hall

A University Theater makeup room

Pages 88-89: Alumni Reunion

Portraits of the University's Nobel laureates in physics, displayed at the Kersten Physics Teaching Center

Recollections
A Few Midway Memories

By Edward W. Rosenheim, A.B. '39, A.M. '46, Ph.D. '53
The David B. and Clara E. Stern Professor Emeritus,
Department of English Language & Literature and the College

It is autumn when most of us come to the University of Chicago for the first time. On campus the leaves are just beginning to change to the gold, scarlet, and brown that will soon glow quietly against the gray walls of the Gothic quadrangles. The squirrels scamper and chatter as they must have done long before the day when Cobb Hall first opened its doors. And the returning students, the relative old-timers, do their own scampering and chattering—a mixed lot, but generally full of talk about what they have been doing and plan to do: enviably energetic and confident, or so they seem to the eyes of the newcomers.

These newcomers themselves have always been a mixed lot, with, it seems, only their newness in common. At this University, graduate students far outnumber undergraduates. They come from every imaginable college or university across the face of the earth, and they have good reason to feel that these quadrangles are where they belong on this October day. But for all of their credentials, they are facing induction into works and ways that are different from whatever they have known before. This might, of course, be said about anyone who has come to the University for the first time. It must certainly be true about that opening day in October, 1892, and about Chicago's original faculty—whose wonderfully promising younger members and famous older ones attested to President Harper's powers of prophecy and of persuasion. To look today at the list of extraordinary men and women who gathered to begin teaching at this new outpost of learning on the raw edge of a brashly booming city is to be reminded that any newcomer is a bit of a pioneer.

Edward W. Rosenheim

John D. Rockefeller and President William Rainey Harper at the University's Decennial Celebration, 1901

Mandel Hall, 1915

But the newcomers who concern us here are the entering freshmen at the University and, more specifically, a certain, rather typical first day of fifty-odd years ago. The scene is Mandel Hall, and there are several hundred of us freshmen gathered in the severe, quasi-Victorian surroundings which do nothing to soothe our collective nervousness. Our sense of assembling in a ritual of welcome does not make the experience any more congenial. We have already been cowed by patronizing advice from older students as well as by the "student handbook," a rather unpleasant little publication which, after setting forth various official rules and practices, has warned us about a list of "traditions and taboos" ("Only lettermen may sit on the C-Bench in front of Cobb Hall," "High school insignia must not be worn on campus," etc., etc.).

Before this uneasy gathering initially appears the Dean of Students, a handsome, mustachioed southerner, almost suspiciously jocular as he reads a list of bland but manifestly crucial announcements. He is succeeded by the Dean of the College (some of us will never distinguish among the nomenclature and functions of the University's myriad deans). This dean is clearly no waster of words. He tells us that he is happy we are here; that he is equally happy the President is here; that he now introduces the President. And the President, who has been seated in a negligent kind of way in a large armchair, now comes unconcernedly to the center of the stage.

It is over sixty years since Robert Hutchins first welcomed a class of newcomers in Mandel Hall, but I have never known an alum from those early days who has forgotten the occasion. Tall, slim, astonishingly handsome, unsmiling, the "Daring Young Man on the Flying Trapeze" (as he was called in a famous article by the late Milton Mayer) stands quietly for a moment behind the rostrum. If ever there was an

Varsity lettermen and dates at the C-Bench, ca. 1950

awed silence, it is our silence before Hutchins speaks the few sentences which, it appears, he spoke each year, and which, over all the decades since, hundreds of us recall verbatim (or so we believe).

"Young ladies and gentlemen," the President begins. "The University of Chicago is not a hotel, although you should be suitably housed and fed here. The University of Chicago is not a social club, although you are clearly at liberty to form congenial friendships here. The University of Chicago is not a gladiatorial arena, although it is reported that there are opportunities, for those so disposed, to engage in or to observe forms of competitive physical endeavor. The University of Chicago is not a Young Men's Christian Association, although I am told it offers various sources of spiritual nourishment for those inclined to invoke them.

"Young ladies and gentlemen," he goes on. "The University of Chicago is a community of scholars. The characteristic activity of such a community is the pursuit of wisdom. It is this activity which characterizes the University of Chicago and which is your reason for being here. It is to membership in this community that I welcome you this morning."

Perhaps I am elevating those words out of all proportion. Perhaps I always have. But, imagine for a moment. You are seventeen years old. You are in a strange place, awkward in your Sunday suit on a weekday morning. Quite possibly you feel homesick, pimply, sinful, or all of the above. At this point nothing in your otherwise laudable past seems very helpful to think about. Your excellent high school record is not reassuring, perhaps because there was more than a hint of social club and gladiatorial arena about your high school. It seems reasonable to imagine that the students around you share your uneasiness, but your chief feeling about them is that they are all much brighter than you are.

President Robert Maynard Hutchins

The University of Chicago campus, 1905

Hull Gate

*Members of the Class of 1897
at their 25th reunion, 1922*

Yet here, in the midst of this painful insecurity, a famous, brilliant, beautiful man has soberly welcomed you into his community, a community of scholars, and has, in effect, proclaimed you to be worthy of his welcome. You can't exactly say that he has made you less anxious, but he has made clear the importance of what you are about to undertake—and even suggested that some of that importance will rub off on you. As you leave Mandel Hall, you suspect you will never forget this moment of welcome to the University. And you are more or less right.

More or less, because, for most of the time during your stay here, there is not much in what you think or do that basically sets you apart from the ordinary run of reasonable mortals. For all the solemnity of our Mandel Hall induction, there is little that is really austere and less that is cloistered about life in this community of scholars. For me, it has been as though Hutchins's words were engraved, handsomely and indelibly, over an archway (Hull Gate perhaps?) which frames a great arena, filled with an open-ended diversity of sights and sounds, people and events. In this arena there is so much variety, vitality, and depth that only the broadest of terms, such as the word "university" itself, is able to embrace what goes on here.

For most of us, then, there are unforgettable chapters of the Chicago experience that seem remote from—even incompatible with—the mission which, Hutchins asserted, defines our identity. Yet it seems to me that there are few of these chapters which are not, in some sense or other, animated by an awareness of that identity.

Let me illustrate. It is some years now since the Class of 1939 celebrated its fiftieth reunion. On that occasion, the members of the class were invited to respond to a questionnaire which asked, among other things, "What experience of your College days at

Chicago do you remember most vividly?"

Now, mind you, the Class of '39 has, even among Chicago graduates, an unusual share of professional, creative, and intellectually committed folk (at least to judge by that same questionnaire). Yet their overwhelming choice of most memorable experience was the 1935 football game at Stagg Field between Ohio State and Chicago's Maroons—the former the nation's top-ranked team, the latter as downtrodden a lot as ever graced the Big Ten (from which Chicago was shortly to depart forever). But on this occasion, half time arrived with Chicago leading Ohio State by two touchdowns, and the game ended with the utterly exhausted Maroons losing by the supremely honorable score of 19 to 13. The achievement was almost single-handedly that of the legendary Jay Berwanger, but surely his indomitable, battered teammates entered their own Valhalla that day. My own point is that the glory of that occasion had something to do with the gallantry and ability of a band of men who were without athletic scholarships, without any form of subvention or sinecure, without a single compromise of academic standards, without a chance to major in physical education or industrial arts—who were, in short, members of a community of scholars.

Perhaps this story makes the notion of a community of scholars only seem precarious and pretentious. I confess that one effect of a career spent in the shelter of such a community is that, while you presumably remain highly alert to the *quality* of teaching and learning, you tend to relax a good bit about precisely who is a scholar and who isn't. You are not, that is, very eager to blackball candidates for admission to your number. Hutchins presumably was content to define the scholar as a pursuer of wisdom; at least I cannot find a more explicit statement of the matter than what he had to say in his welcoming words. And I've come to feel that Hutchins—certainly

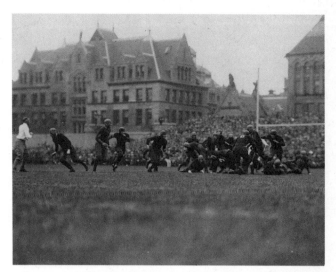

Chicago vs. Illinois, 1924

The University of Chicago campus (Stagg Field in foreground), late 1950s

Albert A. Michelson

John Dewey

never given to bland generalizing, let alone to confusing wisdom with other forms of intellectual attainment—spoke in an awareness that wisdom is pursued in many ways by many kinds of people and that there are scholarly credentials that do not appear on a *curriculum vita*. As I myself have come of age in this University, scholarship has assumed a succession of different meanings, none of which has really cancelled out its predecessors. Let me give some particulars.

In 1971, John Gunther, the popular travel writer-journalist-political analyst, published a modest book called *Chicago Revisited*. In it, Gunther—whose various books with titles such as *Inside Europe* and *Inside Asia* had probed the workings of most major areas of the world—reported affectionately but candidly on what he had discovered on returning to the University of Chicago, from which he had graduated forty-odd years earlier. It's an illuminating, cheerful book, which I happily recommend, but I mention it here only because of its dedication to the memory of two of Gunther's college teachers. These two were Edith Foster Flint and James Weber Linn.

Now I am sure that Gunther knew all about the pantheon of brilliant, original thinkers who have largely accounted for the University's unique distinction from its very earliest days. He knew that any history of thought in this century would give towering prominence to Chicago names such as Michelson, Chamberlin, Dewey, Jacques Loeb, or John Mathews Manley. Moreover, like us undergraduates of the 1930s, he must have been lectured to by the equivalent of such eminences as Harry Gideonse, Louis Wirth, Alfred Emerson, Charles Morris, or that supreme scientist-showman, Anton J. Carlson.

Yet I confess to some pleasure in Gunther's bypassing the various builders of Chicago's greatness to restore a moment of transient glory to figures who, even a score of years ago, must have been all but forgotten. I am pleased because I have my own grateful memories of these two striking teachers. Flint, Ph.B. '97, who taught English (composition, Shakespeare, Introduction to Poetry) for forty-five years, was a majestically massive woman, with a strong, beautiful face that, in its patrician serenity, reminded many of us, not frivolously, of Franklin Roosevelt. We hear a lot about the impossibility of explaining what goes into great teaching, but Flint was so transparently devoted to her students, concerned that they share her joy in literary works, and accordingly patient and resourceful that there seemed to be no great secret in the gratitude she commanded.

James Weber Linn—always called "Teddy"—was an entirely different specimen. Shaggy, gravel-voiced, with a lighted cigarette perpetually hanging from the corner of his mouth, his devotion to the football team was such that he occupied an honorary seat on the bench at all of its games. Yet he was never, I think, uncertain about his mission at the University—which was to teach writing and to do so with all the care, candor, and shrewdness of which he was capable. So that not only John Gunther but Vincent Sheehan, James Farrell, and a good many other professional writers declared their indebtedness to this crusty old Rotarian. No great writer himself, he was a sensitive, thoughtful judge of writing who was likewise patient and generous with any student who shared his respect for language.

I continue somehow to believe that Flint and Linn—with their bachelor's degrees, nugatory publications, and clear preference for the classroom over the library stacks—were in their way valuable members of a community of scholars. I even have a wistful idea that people of their intelligence and devotion might fit into today's tense, trendy, polemical world of humanistic studies—Flint perhaps as an authority on lesser women poets during the Harding administra-

James Weber Linn

A masque called The Gift *celebrates the University's Quarter-Centennial and the dedication of Ida Noyes Hall—Edith Foster Flint as Alma Mater, 1916*

David Grene

tion and Linn as an abrasive semiotics-monger of one sort or another.

From today's perspective, of course, there was something ingenuous about my youthful perception of such long-established classroom favorites as authentic scholars. I have, though, no misgivings about the other teachers—most of them young—who made it clear that a scholar should be not only devoted and curious but discerning, responsible, and, by no means least, abundantly informed. To put it bluntly, and in a somewhat un-Hutchins fashion: through such teachers we discovered what it means to be learned.

I suppose that anyone who went through the College during my years as a student—come to think of it, anyone who has ever gone through the College—can come up with his or her own list of those teachers who truly contributed to their intellectual initiation, who clearly opened vistas of previously unfamiliar knowledge. For decades I have heard such names from scientists, social scientists, humanists, and lawyers—as well as all those who cherish learning although they do not earn a living by it. The lists of such names are not necessarily those of dissertation directors or colleagues, but those who, in the process of teaching undergraduates, succeeded in communicating the excitement and satisfaction of the inquiries to which their own careers were fundamentally devoted.

This fragment of a memoir is certainly not the place for announcing an all-star team, but it is easier to talk of the kind of teacher I have in mind if I cite examples. David Grene, to name one, was for me, and for hundreds of other students interested in the humanities, a teacher of enormous importance. There is so much colorful anecdote surrounding this indelibly Irish classicist—his farm and its livestock, his horsemanship, his gifted offspring, his travels, his friends and enemies, his habits of dressing, lecturing, and socializing, his own anecdotes, his convictions on all imaginable issues—that there is some danger of slighting the central, prodigious gift he has brought to the University for more than fifty years. That gift was clear, at the outset, to the teen-aged students who sat in the twenty-five-year-old Grene's classes. It was the gift of a learning so wide and profound yet accessible that—delighted though we often were by the brilliance of his neckties and his metaphors, or by the bits of horse dung that fell from his boots as he paced about the lecture room—we were never really diverted from our encounter with texts and contexts and the problems and pleasures attaching to them.

If it is good to be welcomed to a community of scholars, it is even more gratifying to be talked to as a peer by a brilliant, intense, but amusing man who seems to assume that his students share his mastery of Greek, Latin, French, and German, and who acts as though, together, we are all simply refreshing our knowledge of the *Republic*, the *Oresteia*, *The Tempest*, the *Leviathan*, or *Ulysses*. Grene's publications, beyond his justly famous translations, are substantial, original, and notably diversified; what he writes and says about literary matters is invariably authoritative and adventurous. But I think I speak for many of his students when I say that we honor him above all as a man deeply, naturally, and confidently involved in a universe of books and ideas, who cheerfully assumed that we were, too.

Although Norman Maclean differed strikingly from Grene in any number of ways, it is perhaps significant that each of them was permanently tempted by a life of natural rusticity that had little directly to do with an academic career. Grene had, early in his life, rejected a promising, full-time vocation as farmer of an ancestral acreage; Maclean was fond of telling how the allure of teaching English barely won out over a career in the Forest Service, where he had many years of summer experience. It just might be that those who arrive in academic life after a difficult choice among tempting alternatives—rather than, say, through life-

Norman Maclean

The Anatomy Building and Cobb Gate from Botany Pond, early 1900s

long, single-minded, pious dedication—become the most valued members of a community of scholars.

There was nothing exotic about Norman Maclean, unless it was his harsh, hesitant, oddly beautiful way of speaking. As with Grene, there were many reasons for cherishing his friendship that had little to do with scholarship: his almost encyclopedic knowledge of and deep joy in forests and rivers; his enthusiasm for sport as participant and spectator; his fascination with the geography of America; his un-apologetically partisan politics; his unending, less-than-innocent delight in people of all sorts. Alongside these obvious, lively qualities, his scholarly achievements, as measured by publication, are modest: an illuminating but almost unnoticed study of the English ode; a brief, quietly revolutionary discussion of a Wordsworth sonnet; an equally quiet but arresting and beautiful essay on *King Lear*—these, and a few other well-wrought articles are products of his early years and hard to associate with the fisherman-philosopher-poet who wrote the magical *A River Runs Through It*.

But, once more, many of us who owe many things to Maclean are probably most in his debt because he helped initiate us into the ways of literary criticism. The Maclean of my generation was a disciple and spokesman of what came to be called the Chicago School of Criticism, that fellowship of scholars who had found the *Poetics* of Aristotle to be uniquely helpful in understanding what goes on in literary works of various kinds and who brought to the judgement of these works an order and conviction that were uncommon in the literary studies of the time. As a student of Richard McKeon and R. S. Crane—who, along with Aristotle, could be safely called the founders of Chicago criticism—Maclean applied their ideas to the virgin territory of whatever he and his undergraduates were reading. Moreover, he pursued his approach with a kind of clarity and buoyancy not

Richard McKeon

entirely shared by his distinguished mentors. Because he made no bones of the fact that this mode of investigation was hotly controversial, we were inducted in yet another way into the community of scholars. For the way of the scholar is, more often than not, an adversarial way—a fact to be frankly recognized and, on the whole, rejoiced in.

Many of Grene's graduate students have become famous in the learned world. Yet he and Maclean have seemed to me that kind of triumphant scholar-teacher whose greatness lies, above all, in their lasting impact upon undergraduates. Now, though, it is time to recognize that the majority of Chicago's students are pursuing graduate or professional programs. In these regions, communication with one's peers—or those one hopes to make one's peers—is in a relatively specialized field of inquiry, and it is not difficult to identify those who, in an obvious sense, conduct their work most successfully. There are the lofty lists of Nobel laureates, members of honorary societies, holders of distinguished chairs and honorary degrees, and various widely publicized discoverers and virtuosi in every art and science. Chicago has far more than an ordinary share of these men and women and this is surely another excellent reason for proudly declaring that we are a community of scholars.

Yet this scholarship that it's so easy to call "advanced" is proportionally hard to understand, even partially, and this is particularly true when it fails to claim attention from any public media—which is most of the time. The satisfactions at this level—apart from the profound satisfactions of investigation itself—lie largely in what can be contributed to a particular professional field, solving its problems, augmenting its common reservoir of information and ideas, adding to its number with the people one has trained.

Again, I hope I can be forgiven for drawing upon my own experience at Chicago in naming one

Nobel laureate Saul Bellow

Nobel laureates Tsung-Dao Lee and Chen Ning Yang, 1957

Arthur Friedman

Helen Harris Perlman, School of Social Service Administration, 1965

more teacher to exemplify the kind of scholar I am now addressing. I select him because, in quite basic ways, he is more typical of scores of Chicago scholars than some more famous men and women and also because I can discuss him with some familiarity and with much affection. Ironically, the late Arthur Friedman, who directed my graduate studies as he did those of a number of more illustrious people, objected to the use of the word "scholar," particularly when it was applied to him. One of the most distinguished authorities of his generation on eighteenth-century literary matters, he insisted on referring to himself—and to comparable experts—as a "student" of these things, although, if pressed, he might admit to being a "specialist" in the writings of Goldsmith (whose works he edited magisterially and whom he knew better than any man alive).

In class Friedman was a bit hesitant. There was rarely any jocularity or small talk in his teaching and, even when he was dealing with Samuel Johnson, he was disinclined to engage in any of the anecdotes that inevitably accompany talk about that great talker. Yet there are a number of us who, to this day, devoutly believe that for graduate studies, Friedman was simply the best teacher one could ever have. A student of his once remarked that "it's not only that Friedman is generous; it's that he has so much to be generous with." Put another way, his generosity consisted in sharing with you everything he knew; and he knew a great deal. As an investigator, a "specialist," he was largely a "loner." His massive edition of Goldsmith and the succeeding edition of Wycherley are almost unique among modern editions of voluminous authors in being entirely the work of a single editor—without benefit of sub-editors, boards, or graduate assistants. But his sense of citizenship was clear, not only in his selfless, sustained concern for teaching but in his record of service to the University for some forty years. As spokesman of the faculty's Committee of the

Council; chairman of the Department of English; gracious, informed, and valued adviser; and quiet encourager of younger colleagues, Friedman reflected a sense of responsibility as great to the community as it was to the principles of specialized research.

This image of the scholar-citizen reminds me that, though I have tried to speak of the various meanings that "scholar" has had for me, I have rather neglected the term "community." When you have been at Chicago for a long time, to be truthful, it's hard to speak of community without sentimentality. Certainly there are occasions and institutions here that invite us to sense our community identity in deep, gratifying ways. We folks on the faculty and staff are likely to celebrate weddings and to memorialize our dead in the comforting beauty of Bond Chapel or the stately shelter of Rockefeller. Our diversions—elegant and frivolous alike—tend to be local affairs, and when we engage, as we are prone to, in civic and political undertakings beyond our doorstep, the University label is more often than not implicitly attached to our efforts.

More seriously, there have been moments of real crisis in which our sense of the University community has supported and guided us. Such a moment occurred in the very early 1950s, when the condition of Hyde Park drove the University to wonder whether it could survive in its traditional location and to consider moving elsewhere, in whole or part. The decision to remain was resolutely adopted and realistically implemented. I do not believe this resolution would have been possible without a powerful sense of community and of mission. This event, like every succeeding expression of the University's confidence in its surroundings, has lent strength and pride to our sense of our role in the tremendous city where we belong.

Then there are wry memories of that period, a score or so years ago, when our existence—precisely

Janice Porter is crowned "Miss U of C" at the 51st Annual Washington Promenade, 1954

Rockefeller Memorial Chapel

Vietnam War protest, 1960s

President Edward H. Levi

as a community of scholars—was threatened by those within our own ranks who held us as somehow culpable for the agony of a sustained, morally dubious war. From the perspective of twenty years or more, this chapter of our history remains lamentable, grateful as we are for the wisdom that led to our surviving it. From the same perspective, the episode has had the virtue of fiercely and quite permanently reminding us that we are indeed a community, a precious and fragile community, whose health depends, in great measure, upon continuing self-awareness and self-examination.

And this, in turn, brings me to a final aspect of the University as a communal scholarly enterprise. This has to do with the fact that principles, policies, and plans within the University of Chicago are ultimately directed to this institution's health as a community. This means that significant decisions are not governed by vogue or expedience or individual "bright ideas" or by politics, internal or external. They are governed by our needs and objectives as a community of scholars, in all the diversity I have tried to suggest is essential to us. Once more, two brief examples.

As provost and then president, Edward Levi had a great many things to worry about—and, being Edward Levi, he worried about them more persistently and more productively than most presidents ever have. Among these worries was evidence—gleaned in part from his innumerable breakfasts with undergraduates—that the students in the College were not very conscious of the University as a whole, and this might mean that there was actually an unnecessary dissociation between the two elements. He was dissatisfied, I think, not because he had some mystic faith in the organic unity of the educational process, but because he found that undergraduates were ignorant of the scholarly work and workers who were largely responsible for the University's greatness—that, surrounded by the resources and activities of a preeminent university, their view of higher education was hard to distinguish from that of a respectable but parochial liberal arts college. They were bogged down, in terms of this memoir of mine, in the academic universe of Linn and Flint.

What seems to be a consequence of Levi's concern was the reorganization of the College into a set of Collegiate Divisions, the virtual disappearance of appointments for exclusively undergraduate teaching, and the widely recognized assumption that to teach in the University usually implied some teaching in its undergraduate program. These changes, with all their curricular implications, were prompted neither by abstract theory nor administrative convenience, but by the notion of the University community in its entirety as a source of strength which it was absurd to ignore.

For a final narrative, I turn to the other end of the academic program and President Hanna Gray's concern about graduate study as it had long been conducted in the University's graduate divisions—and in most, probably all, of the universities across the country. Mrs. Gray—whose scholarly as well as administrative experience lent urgency to her opinion—shared the unhappiness of those (including graduate students themselves) who saw the journey to the doctorate as, too often, an uneconomical and melancholy one—needlessly protracted, solitary, and uncertain. To do something about this situation at Chicago was for her of enormous importance, not only because such circumstances seemed unlikely to produce very lively, confident academics, but because the presence of such lonely people and limp programs was plainly inappropriate to this community of scholars. The commission she appointed to analyze and prescribe for this situation was thorough and imaginative, and its recommendations have resulted in a pattern of graduate study that has been emulated by

Harper Library reading room before renovation, early 1960s

President Hanna Holborn Gray

other institutions. The course of doctoral study at Chicago has been given new economy and orderliness; just as important, it has been enlivened by graduate workshops—flexible, innovative, usually interdisciplinary enterprises which are, in themselves, vigorous manifestations of community. The standards of a graduate education remain unaltered. The experience of graduate study has acquired richness and vitality.

When someone like me has been here for many, many years, he is often asked what important changes have occurred during his stay here. The answer is very hard, for change in a place like Chicago is complicated, difficult to discern and keep track of, still more to assess. Often what one is describing is really changes in oneself—one's sentiments, interests, and perceptions. That is probably what I have been talking about in this discussion of what "community of scholars" has meant for me.

When people ask about changes, they tend to follow up by asking what has remained unchanged. That is when I am tempted to fall back on those words of Robert Hutchins and say that the University remains a community of scholars—but you have read these reflections and they make me a bit uneasy about that formula. So I am inclined to give an answer that goes something like this:

The University is a place that is forever devoted to inquiry and to communicating the results of inquiry, whatever they may be. These are the processes that we call education. The University is a place where all of us take education seriously. But it is also a place where we pursue education with high spirits, with joy. That is why I am grateful to have lived and worked here.

Graduate Workshop in the History of Human Science, 1984